Sea Turtles

Neville Grant

Series Editor
Neville Grant

LONGMAN

Publishing for the Caribbean

Addison Wesley Longman Limited
Edinburgh Gate, Harlow,
Essex CM20 2JE, England
and Associated Companies throughout the world

First published 1996

ISBN 0 582 27786 8

Set in 16pt Newhouse Infant

Printed in Singapore
by Longman Singapore Publishers Pte Ltd

The Publishers' policy is to use paper manufactured from sustainable forests.

Illustrated by Sheila Galbraith

Acknowledgments

We are grateful to the following for permission to reproduce the photographs featured in this book:

Charles and Sandra Hood/Bruce Coleman Ltd (cover); Silvestris/Frank Lane Picture Agency (page7); Mark Newman/Frank Lane Picture Agency (page 9); · Jean-Paul Ferrero/Ardea (page 12); David Hughes/Bruce Coleman Ltd (page 14)

Contents

1 What are turtles?

A turtle is a reptile.
It has a hard shell.

This huge turtle lived a million years ago.
It was four metres long, and was as heavy as a truck.

2 What do turtles look like?

Look at this Green Turtle.

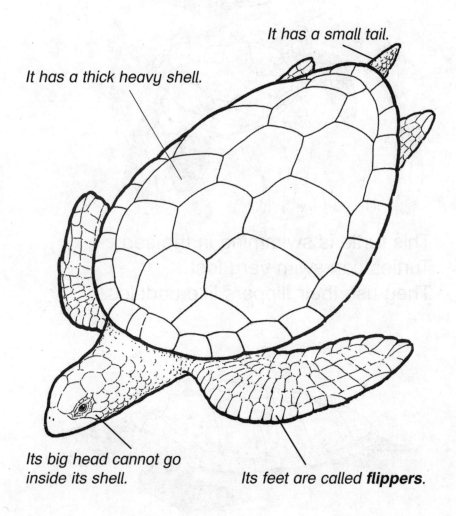

It has a small tail.

It has a thick heavy shell.

Its big head cannot go inside its shell.

Its feet are called **flippers**.

3 How do turtles move?

This turtle is swimming in the sea.
Turtles can swim very fast.
They use their flippers like paddles.

This turtle is on land.
Turtles cannot move very quickly on land.

4 Where do turtles live?

Some turtles live mostly on land.

A Mexican land turtle.

Some turtles live in the sea.

5 Why are turtles important?

Turtles are very beautiful animals.
They are very interesting.
They are useful.

In the old days, sailors used to catch and eat many turtles.
*Many kinds of turtle are now **extinct** because people killed them all.*

6 How long do turtles live?

Some turtles have lived for nearly two hundred years.
Green Turtles live for forty to fifty years.

The Chinese love turtles because they live a long time.
You can still see this turtle in China today – made of stone!

7 How big are turtles?

Some turtles are very small.
The smallest turtles are nine centimetres in length.

This picture shows this turtle's real size.

The largest turtle in the world is the
Leatherback.
These are up to two metres long.
A Leatherback Turtle can be heavier than
seven men!

A Leatherback Turtle with a ten-year-old child.

8 Which is the commonest turtle?

The commonest turtle in the Caribbean is the Green Turtle.
The Green Turtle is one and a half metres long.
A Green Turtle can be heavier than a man or woman.

A Green Turtle swimming near Barbados.

9 What do turtles eat?

Sea turtles eat all these things:

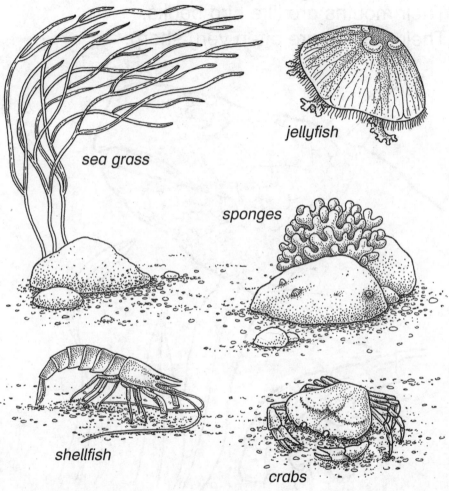

jellyfish

sea grass

sponges

shellfish

crabs

Green Turtles eat shellfish when they are young.
They eat plants when they are older.

10 Do turtles have teeth?

Turtles do not have teeth.
Their mouths are like bird beaks.
Their mouths are often very sharp.

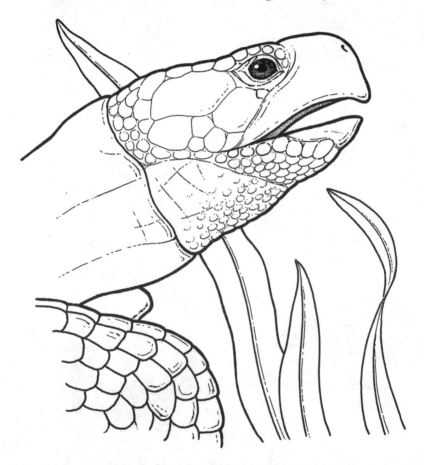

This turtle is waiting to catch a fish in the sea near St Lucia.

11 Where do turtles come from?

Turtles lay their eggs on the beach
between March and August.
They dig holes at night, and lay their eggs
in the holes.
They cover the eggs with sand. Then they
go back to the sea.

A mother Loggerhead Turtle during egg laying. Can you see her eggs?

12 What happens to the eggs?

Turtles lay hundreds of eggs, but not all of
the eggs hatch.
Sometimes sea water spoils the eggs.
Sometimes animals come and eat them.
Sometimes people dig up the eggs and eat
them.

*A mongoose on a beach in Jamaica, looking for turtle
eggs to eat.*

13 What happens when the eggs hatch?

The eggs hatch after six weeks.
The young turtles go down the beach
to the sea.
Birds and crabs catch many of them.

A young Green Turtle hatching on a beach in Tobago.
Turtles come out of the eggs at night when it is safer.

14 Where do young turtles go?

Nobody knows where young turtles go after they reach the sea.
People think they stay in seaweed floating on the sea.

Seabirds and sharks eat many of the young turtles in the sea.

15 How are turtles used?

Many people like eating turtle meat and turtle eggs.
They also kill turtles for their skins, and their beautiful shells.

Most turtles are protected by law, to save them from becoming extinct.
But people still hunt them.
These dead animals were stuffed, and sold to tourists.
The police took them away from the tourists.

16 Why do we need to protect turtles?

Turtles need to be **protected**.
Their numbers are going down.
They are in danger of becoming **extinct**.

Turtle wardens protecting turtles on Matura Beach in Trinidad in the breeding season.
Many countries have laws to protect turtles.

It would be very sad if we killed all the turtles.
Would our lives be better, or worse, if they became extinct?
What do you think?

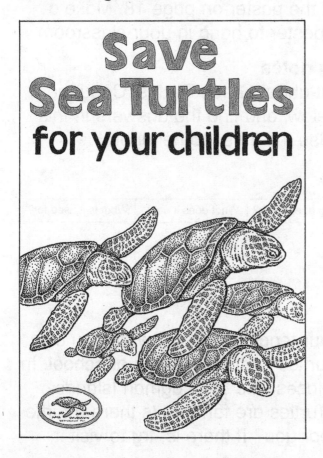

Turtles are in danger all over the world.
This is a poster from Papua New Guinea.

Activities

1   Answer these questions:
    a) What do we use turtles for?
    b) Why do we need to protect turtles?

2   Look at the poster on page 18. Make a
    similar poster to hang in your classroom.

3   **Making notes**
    Find out about Green Turtles. Copy the
    table below, and find the answers in this
    book. Use the index to help you.

The Green Turtle

Length	How long does it live?	What does it eat?	What is it used for?

4   With your teacher, find out what you can
    about turtles near your home or school. In
    some places, like the Cayman Islands,
    Green Turtles are farmed. Is there a turtle
    farm near you? If there is, try to visit it.

Glossary

This book has some new words. Here is a list of them, and their meanings:

extinct   no longer alive. Dinosaurs are extinct. Many animals have become extinct in modern times because of the actions of mankind.

flipper   the part of a turtle's body used for swimming.

protect   guard, keep safe.

reptile   a cold-blooded animal covered in rough skin, like a cayman or snake.

sea grass   long grass growing under the sea.

sponge   a sea animal that lives and grows on a piece of rock or coral.

warden   a guard, someone who looks after people or things.

Index